Wild Everything

Wild Everything

JENNIFER STRUBE

Illustrations by Linda Strube

RESOURCE *Publications* · Eugene, Oregon

Resource Publications
An Imprint of Wipf and Stock Publishers
199 W. 8th Ave., Suite 3
Eugene, OR 97401

www.wipfandstock.com

PAPERBACK ISBN: 978-1-5326-8234-6
HARDCOVER ISBN: 978-1-5326-8235-3
EBOOK ISBN: 978-1-5326-8236-0

Manufactured in the U.S.A.   JUNE 11, 2019

To my daughter,
you are my greatest wild

Poetry is one of the ancient arts,
and it began as did all the fine arts,
within the original wilderness of the earth.

MARY OLIVER

———————————

Contents

Wild You

*Generally speaking, a howling wilderness does not howl:
it is the imagination of the traveler that does the howling.*

Henry David Thoreau

dear child

anything can appear
before you is a world
full of fury and speed
madness and wild and
rush

seasons will change
trees sprout from roots
roots burgeon you
you can place roots
in the fields that most guide you

enter the deepening woods
rest your head on its earth
feel how the forest
invites you to
rest

you are encompassed
from the edge of the heavens
to your very backyard
you are the wild
the world begs to
embrace

brilliant like the ages
are we not oceans
fuller than the earth
are we not giants
oak trees rooted deeply
how then are we not?

are we not rivers
charting our own pathways
are we not sunrise
beaming with new hope
are we not beauty
matching every sunset
how then are we not?

we are not what we remember
we are not what we forget
we are miracles created
from the galaxies before us
we are always
wild everything

before you arrived

I saw you in the smoke
and heard you in the wind
I drank in all your sweetness
in the morning
rain

through dawn-sent dew
I held you close
the scent of
fresh-milled
earth

you were a mystery to me

and now as daylight
trickles down and
evening folds me in
I find you in the
dark of night
the space that won't
let go
the scent of love
on skin

you screamed
and the world
embraced you back
awed by the strength
of your voice
captivated with your
innocence
breathless from your
beauty
your radiance
dissolved them
to tears

when did you stop believing
that this is the truth of you?

eons of love songs

collapse in this moment
thousands of carols
passed from mother to child
lyrics of yore
folksongs from the angels
emerge out of you
my morning lark

tell me what God is like

what she said to you
before you left her loving arms
and descended into mine
secrets that she told you
about life and loss and love
riddles I've forgotten
truths I'm afraid to behold
music I've long silenced
lest I'm overcome with awe

to the redwood

when I look at you
I gaze into the past
love from long ago
pulsing through your veins
strength older than my family tree
roots down to tell
your story

you've seen it all
the epilogue right
from the very start
and still you come
like ancients do
to spread your arms
tonight

don't tell me you're not magic

that stardust doesn't
drip from your fingertips
that angels wings aren't
cresting your back

I see pixie dust
each time you blink
you aren't from here
a transplant from the cherubs
the hallelujah songs you've sung
are anything but faint

the kingfisher

sings her primal tune
and the whole world stops
to gape

here we eavesdrop
here we mimic
here we understand

what if
just for one brave day
we lay down all our masks
open bare our imperfect skin
and let them hear our song?

would they know that we
are feathered queens
heroines of time?

would they let us
wear our birthright honors
tack on capes and
fly?

for the first time

you pulled me into you
two lights melting in
each other's arms
colliding starlight to
stardust

it's as though
from eon's past
we were meant
to make gold together

when stars collide

the universe takes note
an epic collision of
two joining bodies
wobbling to and fro
zealous blasts becoming
violent ripples in time
light years later
these two remain
radiant
rocking
spreading halos
on Earth

to listen

to each other
we must make room
for each other
spread a blanket like a picnicked day
and wrap ourselves in sky

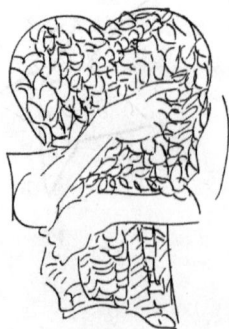

it was the kind of warmth

that makes the orchids drink
soaking up each dewdrop

the kind of moon that makes
the lovers sway
slower than persuasion

the kind of night
where fairy dust
seems just as true as you

where all things make believe
make up everything you are

she believed

yes
she believed in fairy tales
and frogs and searched
for both in her backyard

she was right

she chased the moon

until the stars
returned her
down to earth
for fear she'd miss
the sunset

never

grow up
grow inward
instead
or backward
because

inward and
backward
are true

children trust
where the flowers grow
please stop to
smell the bloom

love has

made you
love will
keep you
love will
let you
shine your
light

run like

the wind will
guide you

leap like
the air will
catch your next fall

harness your
hopes like
the dreams
that propel you

persistent
steadfast
alive

Wild Awe

The clearest way into the Universe
is through a forest wilderness.

JOHN MUIR

you don't have to live in fear
we can make this whole damn life
our own glorious adventure

love,
the explorers

to find a place again

is to find yourself anew
your voice an echo
in an distant song
a play not
long forgotten

sing her back to life
her scene is about to start
the script was written long ago
underneath her skin

her soul is your
double-eared Velveteen
awaiting your embrace

there is a morning coming in

that will struggle to speak softly
whisper your initials in the swallow's song
and set your world to flight

follow her

there are paths

to be found
in pathless woods
pleasure to be had
in the lonely hills
silence
the all-knowing host
spreads a banquet
under your feet
sit
eat
eavesdrop
through the beckoned hush
the rustle of the unturned leaf
the seasons of your life

into the wild

I bumped into myself
the river reflecting my frazzled brow
and circles round my eyes

I cupped a gulp of water
and pressed it my lips

the reflection who returned my gaze
was a she I did not know
a back worn round from grief
shoulders hunched upon her ears
confusion lined her face

was this she me?
I did not know

I came to find the slow
the gift I could not give myself
until the rivers stripped me down
and the forest whispered rest
and the lullaby of birds
assuaged my speeding pulse

I leaned into the waters
and the waters leaned through me
sailing me back to myself

at the campfire

I bring you nothing
but softness
the knit of woven fleece
baskets from my childhood garden
the beating of my pulse

please take heed
please take care

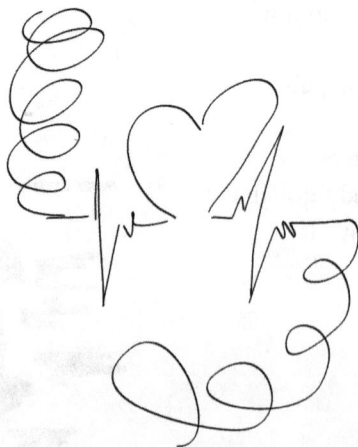

tell everyone

that leaves
are turning
over mountain
peaks
days are
sinking
shorter with
each brazen
sky
earth is
bursting
forth in
hues and
shades
as love
bursts you
awake

grow then

like the wild flower
bring beauty to the places
you never thought could blossom
your splendor an amazement
a wonder unexpected

it's the strangest thing

to return to places
that once held you
back roads that once lost you
cities that once knew your drink
to stand there on the pavement
and smell the freshness of the earth
skin older now
heart softer now
soundtrack cueing now
when they ask you for your name
can you hear it being born?

hidden

terrain that can't be
mapped
by compass or by
crook
it's funny how
life turns
us round

we spend our
days charting
plans and paths
but end up where
we fall
never fully grasping
what lights guide us
what moats float us
and how we are always
home

my conversation with a doe

was unforeseen
the light
flecked in her eyes
fond to greet
insatiably curious
to see and be seen back

she held this gaze
before me
beckoning me to rise
a stance without fear
a gaze without question
reaching into freedom
for everything

these days

keep growing shorter
and the corn keeps growing
longer and my heart
keeps growing fuller
growing old with
you

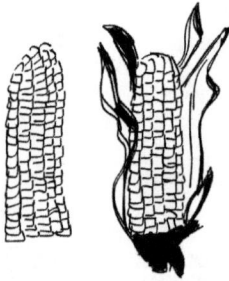

on the coldest of winter nights

in the wildest of wilds
twirled the hearts
of a man and a woman
and their palms folded love into miracles
and their love gathered signs into stars
and the men we deemed wise
told women much wiser
to follow
follow the light

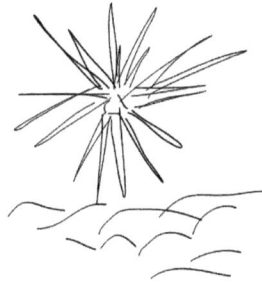

on sunday mornings

I hear it most
the relentless call
to slow
to still
to heed
unspoiled silence

to loose myself
into the woods
and learn
what lost is like

to find my way
back home again
and open hands
to sky

this contact with
the vast beyond
this is how I pray

the wind at his back
the sky in her face
this American girl
with her horses to race
there's a free fall
we are all running to
let's convene there
just me and you

dear mr. petty

at dusk

I sail down
all your rivers
and bathe beneath
your stars
by dawn
I sail into myself
and submerge beneath
the waters
currents tumbling
over me
scrub me
inside out

I become a
riptide
of sediment
and sand
a torrent of
fresh water
diluted with
pink salt

murky be my clear
murky 'til I'm clear

the desert glared me

down
her beige-eyed
stare
hotter than my
veins could
hold

her starkness
asking
questions
of what
I'm hiding
from

the clouds
rolled by
but we
remained
locked gaze spinning
in a sandy haze

untouched
barren
whole

I mistook the silence for solitude

and wandered into purple hills
thickened by God's paint
no one around for miles to come
save the marigolds or poppies

atop the plateau speckled with gold
dust powdered onto my feet
my heels cracked into sand
and heat burst through my skin
a capsuled time
my open mind
mirages circled round my brow
I could not tell what's here or now
my grandma playing Chopin
and my father chopping wood
these scenes played on in tempo
like songs I'd long forgotten

I climbed another boulder
to hear another hymn
more heated rocks reminding
that time would never stop
whirling sand and whirling dust
to dust we shall return
to dust I must return
I find you here in dust

it was cherry blossom season

in Kyoto
which means the shrines
were full of worshipers
and bamboo mats and smoke

of course we sampled
strands of incense
like pilgrims often do
cleansing hands in dragon fountains
leaving shoes at doorstep altars
ringing bells from rope-wrapped towers
clanging gongs with nearby monks

words were few
to make us holy
just candles lit
and fragrance burned
we paused together under trees
and bowed heads to sacred earth
the tint of coloration
expectation of the bloom
our springtime consecration

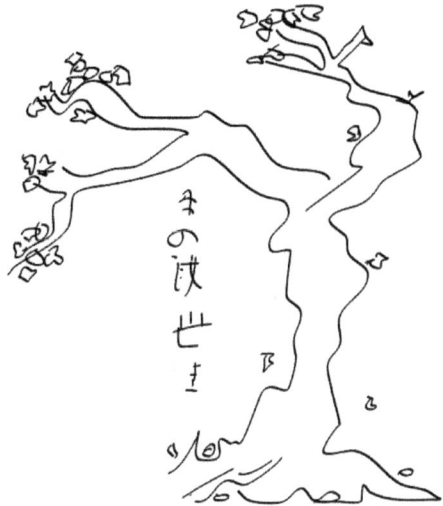

there were those

who came
to worship the sun
and others who came
to study her light
and others who
reflected the glow
back in us

everyone's looking
for a little light to
come down

are we are going

back home
she said

or are we going toward home
he said

so are we walking in circles
they said

until their hearts said
home's right here

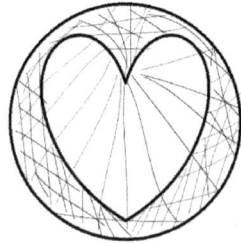

open sky

the perfection concoction
for awe
or angst
the natural elixir
for melancholy

the stunning cocktail
of bare-boned horizons
bare bones you

shake gently
drink deep

Wild Ache

In December and January of 2017–2018,
my hometown of Santa Barbara was ravaged by wildfires
and mudslides. Homes were destroyed and lives were lost.

Nature is neither predictable nor kind. She can be raw
and all-consuming. We stand still at her precipice
and ponder her arduous mysteries.

all my life

I've wanted more
or else why would I
embrace this hysteria?

busy-bodied days of
urgent requests and
inbox full of importance

the list is never-ending

one fall morning
among the leaves
I found all that I had buried
piles of waste under
piles of haste
numb dreams from long ago
strong hopes I feared to hope for
that love I never found
all lay vacant under twigs and stones
awaiting their winter burial

the days were getting shorter
so I returned to the tasks at hand
I couldn't face the slow down
the wonder if it's all been for naught

we long for peace
but is that true
can we stand the deceleration?

when all that remains
under the earth
is the relics of our
childhood selves

and still
we keep on digging

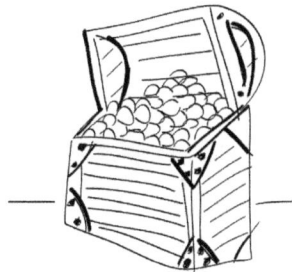

to awake

in the middle of the night
because all that you own
might burn

to knock on your neighbor's door
to alert her of the charge
and check on her recovery
her bosom's cancer burning full
as the flames behind your homes
and you hate the disease
that gives her six months
and the alarms that give you minutes

how many of our days
are we actually dying
how many are we actually safe?

to know of your impending fate
before smoke pours down your throat
and cancer spreads in her chest
to have doctors fight poison with poison
while firemen fall like trees
life presents us with moments of panic
there is no need to search them out
the rest is up to us

there's no segregation

in fire or flood
nature does not discriminate
between black or tall
or white or round
red or blue or birthplace

we are all at it's mercy

it's a crazy thing

to sort your life
into boxes
what to take
what to forget

to know
what can never
be lost

when objects hold history
you clutch love in your palms
fill fast your arms
unclench your fists
and vow to just
let go

when it hits you
when the sky is dark
and the wind howls low
and the land begins to groan
when streets fill with rivers
and rivers float cars
and seas become rafts of salvation

that's when it all makes sense

after the flood
the next day continues
on like it was before
except for last night
when the rains poured
through houses
and the floods buried cars
lifting bodies to roofs

the sun rises still
as teams search and rescue
and birds chirp their songs

that's when it won't make sense
when nature abandons her fawns

the morning after

mist rises from pavements
and sky fills with fog
a yellow-hued dawn sits
disturbingly still
the morning after

a whole world crumbles
a whole town burns
smoke framing sunsets
worthy of Monet
a grace so painstaking
a beauty so broken

why is the land is so
wickedly still
the very morning after?

first it was Katrina

that perked our attention
to which wards hold the
floodgates of justice
I married there a decade later
my love note to a city who drowned

then Houston wept
and Florida whirled
earthquakes in Mexico
and volcanoes in Bali
Sandy and Irma
and Harvey and Mitch
we've been hosting tsunamis
since Thailand at Christmas
while rubble pours down
Japanese streets
as ozone cracks
send polar bears fleeing
dear earth our protector
that we fail to protect
dependably forever
in flux

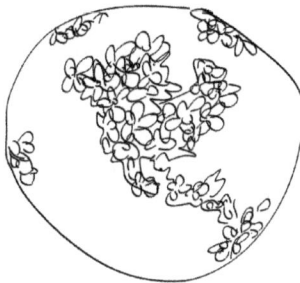

tuck me here

beneath dirt-filled boots
forget here all my power

you think me small
afraid to grow
unknowing my potential

the soil will not swallow me
a sprout that shall not falter

I rise again
again I rise
again
I
rise
anew

in the dead of winter

the week before the birth of our Lord
I watched a squirrel not yet full grown
search the soil for food
her harvest had been late
her childhood short
a few rare months
to spend in frolic
before autumn dropped
her bounty

she dug until the frosty earth
unveiled a single seed
too weak to drag it home
she consumed her find
as the outer shell broke open

I wondered if she ate in haste
or said grace before her meal
did she know this was her final chance
to feast before the snow

to trust that today is enough
or tomorrow will take care of itself
to plan and to store
and to rest on earth
and let life just break you open

Home in
the Wild

In summer 2015, my husband and I embarked on a
2,500 mile road trip to tour nine national parks.

In these wild lands, we encountered wild people—
travelers finding landscapes that matched
the pulse in their veins.

We asked each of them their story
of how they found their homes.

Grand Canyon

inertia was her first response
as to why people settle
down where they do
people don't like change

she told us this over beef stew and cornbread
when the soup matched the
thickness of air
100 degrees at dusk

a headlamp on brow
bandana on neck
she was headed up bright angel trail
the darkness had brought her into this crevice
and the darkness would lead her beyond it

she was anything but inert
making her home in movement
husband by her side
her canteen on her back
a husky guarding her leg

years ago
she bought a one-way ticket
to head west around the world
three months before departure
she learned she was with child
their daughter is now grown
and lives abroad in Sweden

Stockholm resembles Minnesota
the place where we stem from
lakes and trees and a northern feel
people go where they feel familiar
people travel to find the familiar

she sipped her evening coffee
and returned up the path that brought her

Phantom Ranch

they don't pay you for the walking
and the ascending commute is slow
ten miles down and ten miles up
but who gets to work the Grand Canyon
I do that's what I say
I'm a lucky man to work this joint
and that's how I have to tell it

his name was Chuck
with a 70's beard
serving beer at the canyon station
up at four to cook us bacon and hash
sending travelers on their way

I work for a month
then I'm off for a week
the days are long
but whose counting
no toxins here
to blind my eyes
not like my factory days

Hal's fastest ascent was
four hours and change
running straight up the South Rim Trail
then it's back to Phoenix
to his family and kids
his bedroom away from nature

one hundred fifteen
for the daytime heat
and forty degrees by night
his home deep in the crevice
his heart divided by light

Glacier National Park

wherever you live
you'll have 30 close mates
so why not find them out here
I could never find kin in a city
or share my friends with millions
people crowd the land
it's true
air is what lets me breathe

he sat by the river
on a Montana eve
but the silence was far too
commercial for him
he was raised by the good folk
in a hometown of 80
and longed for air round his chest

a pilot
he met the love of his life
by searching for cities with sun
Phoenix seemed warm so he
signed up for Match
and found his love lived in Arizona

I fly to her
she flies to me
the space feels right
together we bridge the sky

stay calm and play dead
that's what Carol's shirt said

a gal in her 60s from Colorado Springs
she stood on the waterfall trail
her flap hat shielded her neck from the sun
her vest patches touting her talents
a staple of khakis and cameras and nets
and hiking poles carved by real chiefs

we are traveling for good
we are nomads you'd say
we stay 'til the itch says go

Carol traded her home for her dream RV
and made Yellowstone her first stomping ground
here she's friends with the moths
and the bison and bulls
but not with the local bear grizzly

that's what the shirt's for
I saw him up close
when all else fails
you play dead
I think the only thing
that keeps one alive
is laying close to the dirt

for me
there is no other place
like Jackson Hole
I just haven't found anything better
except for a corner of Switzerland
but who can afford the Swiss

such were the words of Ivan
bearded and brewing
and brooding and bold
owner of multiple coffee roasts
he came to the States
from the capital of Czech
history chock full of brew masters
America meant freedom
adventure and options
and for these
he headed straight to the West

the towns were too full of laziness
I was lacking ambition
the sun and sand slowed me down
I needed a land to ignite me

he followed his friend to the Wyoming hills
and started his brew in the Tetons
hand-roasting
hand-brewing
hand-building espresso
his coffee can fuel him for days

I grind a few hours
and then pack up and go
the snow builds up
the town shuts down
the energy fuels me to powder

the first time I saw Jackson Hole
I knew it was home
that's where you settle
when it's not settling at all
when it's absolutely love at first sight

Zion

and then there was Lloyd
our waiter at the Thunderbird Diner
home of the homemade pies
Lloyd grew up in Utah
but spent decades in Rochester
working until Kodak went bankrupt
it was 2010 when his job rolled up
along with the lifeblood of his town

those were disturbing times
Lloyd went without pay
for more than 2 years
in search $12.50 an hour
when he couldn't find work
he packed up his bags
and returned to his homeland of Utah

my daughter can tell me
that she's out to play
and I don't have to worry or fret
I can look out the window
or watch down the street
the life here is simple and quiet

Lloyd brought us fried chicken
and potatoes twice baked
when he spoke of the trade-offs of life
back east
Wal-Mart was only 4 miles
out here it's beyond 85

that's all Lloyd could tell us
before he was beckoned away
tables awaiting his omelets
his daughter awaiting her dad
true homemade food in the backlands

Canyonlands

a two-hour drive down an abandoned dirt road
brought us the largest Allosaurus collection

it was closed
or so the sign said
but four hands passed us through
a biology student from UCLA
who came out to the desert to dig
the other—a lover of all things green
who moved west from New York City

this land contradicts
my urban existence
and for that I've fallen in love
when lights go down
your mind sets too
it's like praying alongside the ancients

they spent an hour with us
discussing the theories
of dinosaurs and why they left town

poison water
poison food
flood or natural disaster

each theory sparked questions
rather than truth
but that's how the science goes

they're all compelling
most science is
but the story has to move you
the ones I like most
make the least logical sense
but that lets me fill in the colors

we drove away with golden hues
casting shows of red on the sand
the land lets you fill in the colors
the truth is found under the palette

Bryce Canyon

four hours west from Moab
we camped at the edge of the canyon
over morning bacon
and sausage and brew
we shared a table with a regular joe
we mentioned we were headed
out for the loop
he mumbled he was just passing through

where are you from
and where's home for you?

these were questions with copious answers
adopted from Austria by an American crew
they raised him in South Venezuela
his father led drill teams south of the border
until Las Vegas offered him work

there's options in oil
pops drilled down deep and
blew things up and apparently
did so with style
so our government asked him
to drill to the core
and brought him up to Sin City
I'm in government too
the law enforcement kind
there's plenty to cover in Vegas

in his brown leather bomber
and black metal hat
he dropped his cash on the table
before we could ask
what his pops drilled for
he offered his own version up

they test those bombs
down deep in the earth
don't let them tell you they don't
you didn't hear it here
you won't hear it there
they split atoms under Las Vegas

we finished our casserole
and set off on foot
as he sped away on his Harley
were we walking toward freedom
or walking toward fury
as we descended in the canyon's deep holes?
there's a revolution under our feet
what's the truth at the center of time?

The West
Our Wild

a fictional prose poem
from a semi-true tale

"I'm going hunting in the morning, but I don't want to leave you abandoned," he said, placing the tin cup down on the cedar table. We sat by candlelight, drinking port and speaking of nothing.

This was all new to me.

The cup rested firmly in his hands, the blue speckled paint on the tin matching the sunspots on his wrists. He was nearly twice my age, but that brought an ease to the table. He was both stranger and family in a time when my mother kept asking me to start one, as though kin were something you collected.

"Put down roots," Mom had said.

Planting was not my specialty. Family was not that easy.

He was a rancher. He had spent his skin in leather tannins on a partnership with the soil. Everyone told him to go to college, but he stuck to the dirt instead. He often brought it up in conversation, the fact that he wasn't educated, but he did so with words that only a studied man knew, such as "pejorative" and "effusive."

He should have been profoundly confusing, but he wasn't. He was an earnest man, the now-husband of my widowed mom and the reason we were sent to the woods.

"It's time you accepted Everly. He's not going anywhere and you could learn a lot from this man. Let him take you on his hunt," Mom had said.

Funny, Everly and I were just fine. There was nothing much to accept. He was around, I was back on Mom's couch after a failed relationship, and together we formed a hybrid. I didn't have anything against him; I was just too stubborn to admit it. Plus, Mom had chosen a cowboy this go round, that rugged Stetson-ad type. Not that I looked at my step-dad that way, but his smile was hard to ignore.

He left at daybreak as they all do.

I heard him go but said nothing.

Seconds passed like molasses—it was hard to tell time tucked inside these mountains. The sun didn't peek over the crest until well past daybreak, and when good port has been involved, timeframes got slightly blurry.

By the time I splashed water on my face, the sun was hitting the third mountain crest and not the nearby second. At my feet the sound of the river lapped, splashing every crevice of rock. The local bluebird began his song. A frog sent out a mating call, although I'm pretty sure spring had long passed. But who was I to judge his efforts? At least he was putting himself out there.

I rolled over in my sleeping bag and reached for my day bag, my hand scrambling blindly for all that I had brought. There were the standards: the toothbrush, the journal, the Advil, the eye mask to block the light, the headphones to drown the silence. All things to escape.

What I most wanted was some coffee.

He had placed some coals on the fire and his rifle on the table. It was everything we needed for morning tea and protection.

That was how he was. This was how it was. Always preparing for others in ways the other couldn't accept.

We only had a week.

A week was all we needed.

He was looking for the 12-point buck, the giant that roamed these hills. Legends of this animal began in his grandpa's day, the man who carved this camp. These days no one ever came back to these parts except by horse or foot.

We came on both. He walked. I rode. He lassoed and wrangled and trained. That was the way we moved.

"Dealers in. Time to up the ante and lay down all your cards." He grabbed some pesos from his pocket and threw them on the table, the thick piece of redwood lined full of port and spurs, cards, coins, and wax.

We played poker by candlelight. I still knew nothing of the rules, despite how often I'd played. I could never remember which hand trumped all or when one should purposefully lie.

The horses grazed freely next to us, roaming under the midnight sky. They weren't going anywhere, even though there was everywhere to go. Open fields. Grass-filled meadows. They could have bolted in an instant, but no one runs away from here. This was the land where creatures paused.

Back home, I imagined Mother sitting in front of the television scouring the national debates. She was convinced this was the end of the world where winner takes all, bringing or bankrupting hope.

Out here, the campfire flickered and all else faded away.

"This peso is from 1980," I said, throwing my cards down. I had only three coins left to wager.

"It's too bad you're broke," Everly replied, tossing a bag of nuts my way. "This is our new coin, the real way to trade. Plus it's hard to care if you win or lose when you can eat your gains in a mouthful . . ."

"Nature's first coin. Pistachios. I bet the Greeks traded these." I threw down a nut and my coins.

"1980? Is that an important year to you?"

"It's the year I was born."

"Well, I guess I should have known that."

"I'm mighty old, Everly," I said, throwing two pistachios in mouth. "I only have a few good years left."

"Who lied to you? That person should be jailed. As should the person who taught you to lie." And with that, he laid down four aces.

It was nightfall and way past our bedtime.

At daybreak, we washed the soot off our face, ash from sleeping close to the fire. At mid-day, we scrubbed the dirt off our hands, fingers torn with gathering wood. At night, we night we scrubbed our teeth, our hands now a long lost cause.

In the afternoon, we fished with hook and line.

These were men things to me. My late father always told me that I could never build a barn like he did. My mother always told me not to marry young or have a bosom full of children like she did. I often wondered what all the ruckus was. I could swing a hammer and birth a child if I ever wanted to. My mother ran the children. My father ran the checkbook. A cliché long grown old but seemed to work for them.

Until it didn't.

I had neither children nor a checkbook. I had washed my hands of it all.

"He's thinking about the bite," Everly said of the fish, staring at the line. "Let him think some more."

The fish thought hard and gulped the bait. Before I knew it, Everly was blessing the trout and grilling it for dinner. We ate. We drank. We played some rummy, but by then it was getting late. We washed the fish off our hands and the day off our face and slowly drifted to sleep.

I could not speak of fog. It was one of those nights where I wanted the cloak, the mist that hung low over the river.

Tonight there was no mystery, the sky too clear for shrouds. Buckets of stars holding buckets of stories hung above our brows.

I was never good at constellations.

When we had split, my ex had told me to find direction. "Find your North and call me," he had said. I was never sure if that was an invitation or a favor. Either way, I wasn't calling.

"How do you find North?" I asked Everly.

"Just look for the light that won't move."

"That's my whole life right now; nothing is moving. Everything feels like silt."

"I'm talking stars, kid."

"I'm talking life, Everly. By now, I thought so many things would have fallen into place. Never did I think I'd be lost in the woods with my step-dad, without a job or direction or..."

"Hey now, you aren't lost in the woods," he said, his hand reaching my left shoulder. "The woods never loses anyone. You are right here."

He was always literal. I think that's what Mother saw in him. Her and I were often stuck in metaphors.

"Look," he said. "I think I found a way for you to trust me. I'm going to put a shovel in the ground by this here tree. And in a few hours, we are gonna look up at the sky and right above the shovel will be the North Star. That will be your light that doesn't move."

"And what will that prove?"

"There is place in the world that won't spin."

He threw the shovel into the ground and then set out to clean up camp. The moon above was waxing. Things were growing.

The horses knew it, or so he said. He said many things that I wasn't sure about, like how the deer could predict weather two weeks out. Or how fish could see us through the river so you hunt behind their gaze. He said that mules are selfish which makes them safer to ride, because they take care of themselves and not you. You want a selfish animal on terrain like this to keep their feet most stable.

I grew up with horses. Granted, my saddle had no horn, just polished English gear that rode the East Coast circuit. His horses were named after field grains or drinks. Whisky. Tonic. He roped his horses from the pastures and used them to carry supplies. I jumped mine over well-manicured poles while well-manicured men judged me.

Tonight, there was no need for ribbons. There was little need for anything in these parts, save a knife to gut the fish and a shovel to find a star.

I wasn't convinced he'd found it.

"You sleep alright?" I heard him say, before I was even awake. I could smell the brew of his coffee and the hints of freshly burned wood.

"Very well, I reckon. Nothing like the smell of cedar."

I was starting to talk like him, although I'd never admit it. It had only been three days out here on the land and everything was slowing down, in the way nature rocks you to safety.

I rolled out my sleeping bag and stepped outside. The sun was starting to crest the hill and a single cloud hovered over the tip of the peak. The sun started her day early here, but she didn't stop Everly in his tracks.

He was already gone before I could thank him for the coffee. Each morning in these woods, he left alone in search of the stag. I wasn't much of a hunter, so he knew the invitation was a lost cause. Yet, I wasn't exactly a vegetarian either. I couldn't kill an animal, but I had no problem eating meat. The stag he'd find would be his meals for the approaching winter.

Mother was apparently embracing venison.

I passed the day by the river. Even with the slowing time, evening came before I knew it, before I knew much of anything.

That night, we had a waxing moon. Signs said things were growing.

Tonight, there were no accolades. All we needed was a knife to gut the fish and a shovel to find the star.

I still wasn't convinced he had found it.

"How long are you gonna analyze this? North is as easy as it gets."

"Is that right?"

"You find direction, pitch a shovel, and rest easy from there. And if you are wrong, you simply move the shovel. Here, come sleep under the stars. The meteors are set to fall and maybe you can find your message."

"I'm fine inside the cabin. You let me know what the stars say," I said.

"Suit yourself. I'll let you decide which frightens you most—finding stars or missing them. You have lots of choices. You always do."

Everything was abundance, even when it wasn't. This was the season of almost, the temporary, the links on a chain that joined for a moment before they break. Almost was everywhere in the air, the turn of the leaves, the fall of the old foliage. Everything was almost finished.

"Can I ask you a personal question?" he said as he spread out his blanket by the campfire. "As a school girl, did you always do your homework?"

"Why not?" I replied.

"I got all D's and F's. The science teacher made a deal with me just so I could get through his class. I couldn't stand that guy. I figured that was a sign to skip the formulas and head to the land. That's where the real truth is."

I went to the river for water to boil, watching the impurities bubble up to the surface. I added tea and felt the clarity press on my lips. It awoke me for the briefest moment.

It was morning, and he was fast at work. He could plan his days without a calendar simply by watching the sun. Dawn to me felt like endless stretch of time, thousands of seconds before me.

I set out to write while he started fixing the horses, the sound of the tack clanging against the metal of the girths. I pounded my pen on the paper. The horses pounded their hoofs in the dirt. I got stuck in my head the way dirt stuck to his fingers. Both were constant. I saw hypotheticals; he saw projects: firewood to be gathered, the tent deconstructed, the shower bucket filled.

I dreamed. He acted. Such was the lay of the land.

He coined me educated; I found him smart.

"Every day I'm learning," Everly told me last night. "This land is always talking to me. There is so much still I'm dumbfounded by, but I'm curious."

I'd quit learning for pleasure in undergrad, despite passing my doctoral comps. It's amazing how much school you can do without thought.

"I think I graduated from high school," he said. "I'm not sure. I skipped the ceremony so I never knew if my name was announced."

We set out on a hike following the trail of tangled trees.

"The manzanitas are all twisted up," he said. "Looks like lighting struck them. Must be a sign from the gods to keep moving."

"Or the God."

"Whatever you wish to call it. You bless God before eating the trout. I'll thank the trout for trading his life for our dinner. You see God in the tree. I see the tree speaking direct."

"Sounds feasible."

We walked for hours without spotting an animal, mostly in silence. We passed through forests of pines, trunks so high they pointed past ourselves.

"Do you know what time it is? It's time for you to believe we've found the North Star. Let's head back to camp before it gets too dark and throw down the shovel."

After dinner around the fire, it was only a matter of time before the conversation turned to love. Perhaps it was the vintage port, love's pure siren call, the muse when no one else pauses. Such is the lure of romance and wine; neither leave each other out of the conversation for long.

"When I was young, I'd push away what was right in front of me and then want what I can't have. Do you ever do that?" he asked.

"Perhaps. Maybe I long for complication. I once know a woman who had a thirty-year partner. They were married for three months and the week after their honeymoon, he had an affair with his ex. When she found out, she ripped up the marriage contract and threw it on the table, screaming, 'I divorce you! I divorce you! I divorce you!' They've been inseparable ever since."

"I guess that's one way to do it."

"She says it's more honest. She gets to decide to stay each day."

"Well, there is something to be said about nothing binding you to anyone but choice."

In the distance, I heard a sputter in the bushes. Rattlesnakes were common in these parts, as were bears. Perhaps it was his nearby rifle or the snakeskin on the table next to the port, a decoration of sorts. Either way, I knew we'd be safe tonight.

He left at dawn to resume the hunt. I asked if I could join him.

"I've got lasers for eyes," I said. "I can spot anything you need, not that I'll tell you if I see the stag."

"You can come, but we have to go downwind or the deer will smell us. Natural geniuses they are."

There were deer tracks and bear markings on the path, but simply no sight of others. The ranger station stood further across the river, but no one even bothered to stock the station with a ranger anymore. Times were changing. No one comes to these parts much anymore.

"The deer still do. You see these footprints? They have crossed the migration trail. The rains must be starting tomorrow. Then they'll begin to move. The doe will leave first with her children.

"Where to?"

"Well, they make their own switchbacks over and through these hills. They go over the mountain and down again, then over the next mountain and out.

We hiked up that waterfall canyon to get to the apex fishing pool, naming each tree we passed. The White Fur. The Gregorian Oak that smells like vanilla. The Ponderosa Pine. We walked for what seemed like hours through leaves. Time kept dripping here, as did the fish. But apparently not the stag or the rain.

The search for the buck left us drenched, as we trenched through a rain that wouldn't quit. While the transistor had predicted only a few stray showers, the high mountains were completely covered in snow. We were only at 6000 feet when the hail pellets started to pound. We set up shop in the cabin and decided to wait out the storm.

"I noticed that the light was on when I got back. I turned it off to conserve the brightness, in case we need it for tonight."

"Sorry, that was my fault. I forgot to turn it off."

He didn't comment, in a season when he always had something to say. I poured us tea. He drank green herbs, and I drank Earl Grey.

We sat on the wooden benches playing cards until the moon rose, then the oil came out for him to shine up his gun.

I had never seen a pistol up close, nor a knife, nor had eaten meat with the person who had taken the animal's life. Nor thanked the animal for his sacrifice. We ate venison from last spring's kill, wrapped in warmed corn tortillas.

Perhaps it the drenching rain that made me feel small, like a shrunken version of myself, but we stood together in the dark of the cabin, me with my journal, him polishing guns. And though he was family, for a moment, I wondered what the hell I was doing in a shack next to rifles and saws. I was a liberal, a pacifist, an academic.

The wind howled outside. He kept asking where I was going to sleep—checking on the bedding to see where I wanted to be.

I wanted to be alone.

It was dark after all. The cabin had a single corner window that barely let light in by day. I noticed it was covered by a spider web. It was the first sign of uncleanliness I had seen at the camp since we arrived. Everything had seen pristine up 'til now, even in the wild.

He had seemed pristine.

He brought out the chess board. He made some moves that let me win but was flustered when I did. I suddenly couldn't understand what Mother saw in him.

The next day he was gone again. I tried to imagine what would happen if he didn't return. I knew how to make a fire, but that was the end of my survival skills. I spent the day wondering how I'd ever get out of this place if I lost him. I was used to traveling alone or with my partner. I wasn't used to depending on my step-dad.

Finally, he came down from the forest.

"I was thinking on my return how you are the perfect woman. Your mother raised you right. Your life is going to pan out just fine."

"You know these woods makes people crazy, casting all kinds of dewy light on people's faces."

"Do I look dewy to you?"

"Here, use my soap to wash your face."

"What for?" he said. "This skin hasn't seen soap in ten years."

"You don't wash?"

"My face I don't. I throw soap in all the important places."

I shrugged it off, the way children do when you ask them a question and they don't know the answer. "Do you believe in God?" I asked.

"I believe in something, but what's that got to do with soap?"

"Everything."

"Oh, you are one of those holy toters, aren't you . . ."

"It was a silly question. You don't believe in soap, why would you believe in God?"

"Now, now, I said my face hasn't seen soap in ten years. Seeing and believing—those are two different stories."

"Are they?"

"Yes, but why so philosophical out here in the woods. Here you just notice what is."

With that he dug his shovel into the ground in the middle of camp. "Stand right there and look up."

This was the fourth time he'd done this. Nevertheless, I looked up and saw a star, a non-descript, twinkling little star.

"There it is," he said.

"There?"

"I've been tracking it all night. That's the one that won't move."

I remained silent.

"Now, I can pitch all the shovels I want into this ground, but you still don't buy it. You say you want direction, for the world to stop spinning. Well, all you want is staring right at you, and you still don't believe it. Seeing North is nothing to you."

Maybe he was right. Perhaps I didn't believe him. It all seemed too easy, but there was no admitting that.

"How sure are you that's Polaris?"

"Sure? I'm 110 percent sure. But my certainty can't make you decide. It's the same with soap. I don't believe in it, but that's not enough for you."

"It's getting late for such questions."

"Look at you, cutting off the philosophical. Okay, let's go to the table. You game for another round of poker?"

"I think I ran out of all my Mexican pesos for tonight."

"There's always more to go around."

"In your world that's very true."

84

On our last day at camp, the snow started falling before my eyes opened. He was up already, organizing tarps and towels, putting perishables away in the pantry.

"Would you like to join me in the cabin for some coffee?"

The cabin was a burrowing hole for impending blizzards. It was a cross between a wilderness lodge and the dreamy shack of my dreams. The cedar logs stood vertically and on the walls were a mixture of tools and skins. A cast iron pot hung next to a tripod. Coleman lamps stood next to stacks of poker decks. There was a tin guitar case filled with copper bullets. In the corner stood two fishing poles and firewood, plus a barometer, compass, and a clock which died years ago. Two anvils hung crisscrossed over what appeared to be an old chainsaw link. Bike tires were stuffed in the corner next to a fringed leather jacket and a shaving mirror. And that was just the first wall.

The opposing wall seemed more for storage and posterity. A wheelbarrow full of chopped cedar. A first-aid kit and a few more bedrolls. Two horse halters, a rain coat, and another mirror—this one larger. A single ladder led up to the sleeping loft, full of bed padding and horse blankets. Downstairs at the base of the ladder was a wood burning stove and a simple wooden table, no doubt built by his father.

He made the breakfast, eggs with rice.

"Thank you for cooking."

"Thank you for your company."

It was always that way with him. As much angst as I felt, I was always received with kindness. I wasn't sure what the angst was about anyway, save maybe this: Mother had finally found a man to treat her right. A handsome one at that. And here I was mid-thirties, still searching for my buck.

"Women call the shots. They decide when and where things happen. You can have the candlelight dinners and romantic words but at the end of the day—it's the women who decide the plot."

"Where'd you get this theory from?"

"I don't make the theories. I just observe nature. The bulls and bucks will go around fighting each other and sure, it's impressive to the ladies. But at the end of the day, if the doe doesn't bat an eye, it's all for naut. The women clear the way."

"So if you see a doe solo . . . ?"

"She chose it that way. Ain't no such thing as a desperate doe. She's never on the hunt."

"Why do you think animals can predict the future and people can't?"

"We are further removed from our instincts. But women aren't. These does will hightail it out of these hills well before the bucks will. They are on it. Just look."

Across the river stood an elegant deer, standing by the bank alone.

"Wait here," he said. "Where there's a single doe, there's often a male behind. Bucks follow the barren females. If they make it out together, by springtime, she will have a fawn.

That night we packed up camp. We would leave with the dawn to follow the does over the mountain before the impending storm. For this season, there would be no stag.

"Where to next, Everly?"

"Home is out here on the range. If the misses says so."

"Look at you and the cowboy songs."

"This land don't lie. It's never failed me once." He handed me the shovel. "I'm going home to the woman I love. It's your turn. Find your North."

Gratitudes

Forever grateful to my mother for her bravery
in life and for sharing her art with me.

To my husband, my eternally favorite muse
and confidant. Thank you for exploring the
world with me and always returning me to sunshine.
You are my greatest natural wonder.

To my child, you are starlight incarnate. I can't
wait to see your wings.

To my hometown of Montecito, no fire or flood
will contain you. Again, you rise.

www.ingramcontent.com/pod-product-compliance
Lightning Source LLC
Chambersburg PA
CBHW062015040426
42447CB00010B/2022